The Goat

or

Who is Sylvia?

Edward Albee was born on 12 March, 1928, and began writing plays thirty years later. His plays include *The Zoo Story* (1958); *The American Dream* (1960); *Who's Afraid of Virginia Woolf* (1961–2, Tony Award); *Tiny Alice* (1964); *A Delicate Balance* (1966, Pulitzer Prize; 1996, Tony Award); *All Over* (1971); *Seascape* (1974, Pulitzer Prize); *The Lady From Dubuque* (1977–8); *The Man Who Had Three Arms* (1981); *Finding The Sun* (1982); *Marriage Play* (1986–7); *Three Tall Women* (1991, Pulitzer Prize); *Fragments* (1993); *The Play About The Baby* (1997); *The Goat Or, Who Is Sylvia?* (2000, 2002 Tony Award) and *Occupant* (2001). He is a member of the Dramatists Guild Council, and President of The Edward F. Albee Foundation. He was awarded the Gold Medal in Drama from the American Academy and Institute of Arts and Letters in 1980, and in 1996 received the Kennedy Center Honors and the National Medal of Arts.

The Goat

or

Who is Sylvia?

(Notes toward a definition of tragedy)

by

Edward Albee

Methuen Drama

Published by Methuen 2004

3 5 7 9 10 8 6 4

First published in the USA in 2003 by The Overlook Press,
Peter Mayer Publishers, Inc., New York

First published in the UK in 2004
Methuen Publishing Limited,
215 Vauxhall Bridge Road,
London SW1V 1EJ

Methuen Publishing Limited Reg. No. 3543167

A CIP catalogue record for this book is available from the British Library.

ISBN 0 413 77385 X

Typeset by SX Composing DTP, Rayleigh, Essex
Printed and bound in Great Britain by
Cox & Wyman Ltd, Reading, Berkshire

The Goat

for Liz McCann – because

The Goat or Who is Sylvia? received its world premiere in New York City on 10 March 2002 at the Golden Theatre, produced by Elizabeth Ireland McCann, Daryl Roth, Carole Shorenstein Hays, Terry Allen Kramer, Scott Rudin, Bob Boyett, Scott Nederlander and Sine/ZPI. The cast was as follows:

Stevie	Mercedes Ruehl
Martin	Bill Pullman
Ross	Stephen Rowe
Billy	Jeffrey Carlson

On 13 September 2002, the roles of **Stevie** and **Martin** were taken over by Sally Field and Bill Irwin respectively.

Directed by David Esbjornson
Set design by John Arnone
Costume design by Elizabeth Hope Clancy
Lighting design by Kenneth Posner
Sound design by Mark Bennett

The Goat or Who is Sylvia? received its UK premiere at the Almeida Theatre on 22 January 2004 with the following cast:

Stevie	Kate Fahy
Martin	Jonathan Pryce
Ross	Matthew Marsh
Billy	Eddie Redmayne

Directed by Anthony Page
Design by Hildegard Bechtler
Lighting by Peter Mumford
Sound by Matthew Berry

Scene One

The living room.

Stevie *on-stage, arranging flowers.*

Stevie (*calling off-stage*)   What time are they coming? (*No response.*) Martin? What time are they coming?

Martin (*off-stage*)   What? (*Entering.*) What?

Stevie (*a little smile; a slowish statement*)   What . . . time . . . are . . . they . . . coming?

Martin   Who? (*Recalling.*) Oh! Oh. (*Looks at watch.*) Soon; very soon. Why can't I remember anything?

Stevie (*finishing flowers*)   Why can't you remember? Are you going to water these? (*Indicates.*)

Martin (*looks down*) Hm? (*Back up.*) Yes, I guess so. Anything; nothing; can't remember a thing. This morning – so far! – I couldn't remember where I'd put the new head for the razor; I couldn't recall Ross's son's name – still can't, two cards in my jacket make no sense to me whatever, and I'm not sure I know why I came in here.

Stevie   Todd.

Martin   What?

Stevie   Ross's son is called Todd.

Martin (*slaps his forehead*)   Right! Why the flowers?

Stevie   To brighten up the corner . . .

Martin   . . . where you *are*? Where *I* am?

Stevie   . . . where you'll probably be sitting, to make the cameras happy.

Martin (*smelling the flowers*)   What are they?

Stevie   Cameras?

Martin   No; these.

Stevie   Ranunculus. I. (*Then.*) I: ranunculi.

Martin   Pretty. Why don't they smell?

Stevie   They're secretive; probably too subtle for your forgetful nose.

Martin (*shakes his head, mock concern*)   Every sense going! Taste next! Touch; hearing. Hah! Hearing!

Stevie   What?

Martin   What?

Stevie   And to think you're only fifty. Did you find it?

Martin   What?

Stevie   The new head for the razor.

Martin   Right! A new head! I'll need that next – the whole thing.

Stevie   Why did you want to remember Todd's name?

Martin   Well, to begin with, I shouldn't be forgetting it, and when Ross shows up and he asks about Billy I can't say 'He's fine, how's . . . you know . . . *your* son . . . '

Stevie   Todd.

Martin   Todd. 'How's old Todd?'

Stevie   Young Todd.

Martin   Yes. It's the little slips.

Stevie   I wouldn't worry about it. Are you going to offer them stuff? Coffee? Beer?

Martin (*preoccupied*)   Probably. Do you think it means anything?

Stevie   I don't know what 'it' is.

Martin   That I can't remember anything.

Stevie   Probably not: you have too much to remember, that's all. You could go in for a check-up . . . if you can remember our doctor's name.

Martin (*nailing it*)   Percy!

Stevie   Right!

Martin (*to himself*)   Who could forget that? Nobody has a doctor named Percy. (*To Stevie.*) What's the matter with me?

Stevie   You're fifty.

Martin   No; more than that.

Stevie   The old foreboding? The sense that everything going right is a sure sign that everything's going wrong, of all the awful to come? All that?

Martin (*rueful*)   Probably. Why did I come in here?

Stevie   I heard you in the hall; I called you.

Martin   Aha.

Stevie   What's my *name*?

Martin   Pardon?

Stevie   Who *am* I? Who am *I*?

Martin (*acted*)   You're the love of my life, the mother of my handsome and worrisome son, my playmate, my cook, my bottle-washer. Do you?

Stevie   What?

Martin   Wash my bottles?

Stevie (*puzzles it*)   Not as a habit. I may have – washed one of your bottles. Do you have bottles?

Martin   Everyone has bottles.

Stevie   Right. But what's my *name*?

Martin (*pretending confusion*)   Uh . . . Stevie?

Stevie   Good. Will this be a long one?

Martin   A long what?

Stevie   Interview.

Martin   The usual, I guess. Ross said it wasn't going to be a feature – sort of a catch-up.

Stevie   On your fiftieth.

Martin (*nods*)   On my fiftieth. I wonder if I should tell him that my mind's going? If I can remember.

Stevie (*laughs; hugs him from behind*)   Your mind's not going.

Martin   My what?

Stevie   Your mind, darling; it's not going . . . anywhere.

Martin (*serious*)   Am I too young for Alzheimer's?

Stevie   Probably. Isn't it nice to be too young for something?

Martin (*mind elsewhere*)   Um-hum.

Stevie   The joke is, if you can remember what it's called you don't have it.

Martin   Have what?

Stevie   Alz . . . (*They both laugh; he kisses her forehead.*) Oh, you know how to turn a girl on! Forehead kisses! (*Sniffs him.*) Where have you been?

Martin (*releases her; preoccupied*)   What time are they coming?

Stevie   Soon, you said; very soon.

Martin   I did? Good.

Stevie   Did you find it?

Martin   What?

Stevie   The head for your razor.

Martin   No; it's around somewhere. (*Fishes in a pocket, brings out cards.*) But these! Now these! What the hell are these?! 'Basic Services, Limited.' Basic Services, Limited?? Limited to what?! (*The other card.*) 'Clarissa Atherton.' (*Shrugs.*) Clarissa Atherton? No number, no . . . internet thing? Clarissa Atherton?

Stevie   Basic services? Clarissa Atherton, basic services?

Martin   Hm? Every time someone gives me one of these, I know I'm supposed to give them one back, and I don't have them. It's embarrassing.

Stevie   I've told you to have them made . . . cards.

Martin   I don't want to.

Stevie   Then don't. Who is she?

Martin   Who?

Stevie   Clarissa Atherton, basic services. Does she smell funny?

Martin   I don't know. (*Afterthought.*) I don't know who she is, as far as I know. Where were we this week?

Stevie (*overly casual; stretches*)   Oh, it doesn't matter, sweetie. If you're seeing this Atherton woman, this . . . dominatrix . . . who smells funny . . .

Martin   How could I be seeing her – whoever she is? There's nothing on the card. Dominatrix?!

Stevie   Why not?

Martin   Maybe you know things I don't.

Stevie   Maybe.

Martin   And I probably know one or two things *you* don't.

Stevie   It evens out.

Martin   Yes. Do I look okay?

Stevie   For the TV? Yes.

Martin   Yes. (*Turning.*) Really?

Stevie   I said: yes; fine. (*Indicates.*) The old prep school tie?

Martin (*genuine, as he looks*)   Is it? Oh, yeah; so it is.

Stevie (*not letting him have it*)   *No* one puts on their prep school tie by accident. *No* one.

Martin (*considers*)   What if you can't remember that's what it is?

Stevie   *No* one! If you do get Alzheimer's, and you get to the stage you don't know who *I* am, who *Billy* is, who *you* are, for that matter . . .

Martin   Billy?

Stevie (*laughs*)   Stop it! When you get to the point you can't remember anything, someone will hand you *that* (*Indicates his tie.*) and you'll look at it and you'll say (*Terrible imitation of aged man.*) 'Ahhhhh! My prep school tie! My prep school tie!'

They chuckle; the doorbell rings/chimes.

Martin   Ah! Doom time!

Stevie (*quite matter-of-fact*)   If you *are* seeing that woman, I think we'd better talk about it.

Martin (*stop. Long pause; matter-of-fact*)   If I *were* . . . we *would*.

Stevie (*as offhand as possible*)   If not the dominatrix, then some blonde half your age, some . . . chippie, as they used to call them . . .

Martin   . . . or, worst of all, someone just like you? As bright; as resourceful; as intrepid; . . . merely . . . new?

Stevie (*warm smile; shake of head*)   You win 'em all, don't you.

Martin (*same smile*)   Enough.

Door again. The next several speeches are done in a greatly exaggerated Noël Coward play manner: English accents, flamboyant gestures.

Stevie   Something's going on, isn't it?!

Martin   Yes! I've fallen in love!

Stevie   I knew it!

Martin   Hopelessly!

Stevie   I knew it!

Martin   I fought against it!

Stevie   Oh, you poor darling!

Martin   Fought hard!

Stevie   I suppose you'd better tell me!

Martin   I can't! I can't!

Stevie   Tell me! Tell me!

Martin   Her name is Sylvia!

Stevie   Sylvia? Who is Sylvia?

Martin   She's a goat, Sylvia is a goat! (*Acting manner dropped; normal tone now; serious, flat.*) She's a goat.

Stevie   (*long pause; she stares, finally smiles. Giggles, chortles, moves towards the hall; normal tone*)   You're too much! (*Exits.*)

Martin   I am? (*Shrugs; to himself.*) You try to *tell* them; you try to be *honest*. What do they do? They laugh at you. (*Vicious imitation.*) 'You're too much!' (*Thinks about it.*) I suppose I am.

Ross   Hey, honey.

Stevie   Hi, Ross. (**Ross** *enters with* **Stevie**.)

Ross   Hello there, old man!

Martin   I'm fifty!

Ross   It's a term of endearment. Nice flowers.

Martin   It is?

Ross   What? What is?

Martin   'Hello there, old man.' Ranunculi.

Ross   Pardon?

Stevie   The proper plural of ranunculus – the flowers, according to old Martin here.

Martin   Some say Ranunculuses, but that sounds wrong, even though it's probably perfectly acceptable.

Ross (*not interested*)   Aha! Let's move that chair over to the . . . whatever they are . . . the flowers. (*To* **Martin**.) Are you happy in that chair?

Martin   Am I happy in it? I don't even know if I've ever sat in it. (*To Stevie.*) Have I? Have I ever sat in it?

Stevie   You just did and you sat in it the last time Ross did the programme with you.

Ross   That's *right!*

Martin   Yes . . . but was I happy? Did I sit there and did contentment bathe me in its warm light?

Ross   You got me, fella.

Stevie   Yes; contentment fell; you sat there and I watched it bathe you in its warm light. I've got to go.

Martin   Where are you going?

Stevie (*no information*)   Out.

Martin   Are we in tonight?

Stevie   Yes. I think Billy's going out.

Martin   Naturally!

Stevie   We're in. (*Glee.*) TV time! I'm getting my hair done, and then I thought I'd stop by the feed store. (*Exits, giggling.*)

Ross   By *what*? She's going to stop by *what*?

Martin (*staring after her*)   Nothing; nowhere. (*To Ross.*) No crew?

Ross   Just me this time – the old hand-held. (*Indicates camera.*) You ready for the chair?

Martin (*sing-song*)   Ha, ha. (*Suddenly remembering.*) How's old *Todd*?!

Ross   'Old Todd?'

Martin   You know: old *Todd*!

Ross   You mean my baby son who just last week it seems I dandled on my knee? *That* old Todd?

Martin   Lovely word – dandled. Yes: *that* old Todd.

Ross   Who I cannot accept having become eighteen?

Martin   Whom.

Ross   Maybe.

Martin   Yes; that one. Can any of us? Ever?

Ross   Pushing me further into middle age?

Martin   Yes; that one.

Ross (*offhand*)   He's okay. (*Laughs.*) He asked me last week – first time since he was four, or something – why he didn't have a brother, or a sister, or whatever – why April and I never had another kid.

Martin   April, May, June – the pastel months. You name girl babies after them.

Ross (*doesn't care*)   Right. (*Does care.*) I told him if you do it right the first time why take a chance on another.

Martin   Did he like that one?

Ross   Seemed to. Of course, I could have told him the whole graduating class got together and vowed that we would all have only one kid each – keep the population down. Speaking of which, how's Billy? How's *yours – your* one and only?

Martin (*attempted throwaway tone*)   Ohhhh, seventeen last week – didn't Todd come to the party? No, I guess he didn't. Real cute kid, Billy, bright as you'd ever want, gay as the nineties.

Ross   Passing phase. Have you had the old serious talk?

Martin   The 'you'll get over it once you meet the right girl' lecture? Nah, I'm too smart for that, so's he, so's Billy. I told him to be sure. Says he's sure; loves it, he says.

Ross   Well, of course he loves it; he's getting laid, for God's sake! Don't worry about him.

Martin   Who?

Ross   Billy! Seventeen; it's a phase.

Martin   Like the moon, eh?

Ross   He'll straighten out – to make a pun. (*To quash the subject.*) Billy'll come out of it; he'll be okay.

Martin (*reassuring if a bit patronising*)   Sure.

Ross   Voice test? Phone off?

Martin   I assume Stevie did it.

Ross   I hear a kind of . . . rushing sound, like a . . . whooooosh!, or . . . wings, or something.

Martin   It's probably the Eumenides.

Ross   More like the dishwasher. There; it stopped.

Martin   Then it probably wasn't the Eumenides: they don't stop.

Ross (*agreeing*)   They go right on.

Martin   Right.

Ross   Why is Stevie going to the feed store?

Martin   She isn't.

Ross   Then why did she . . .

Martin   It's a joke.

Ross   A standing joke?

Martin   No, a new one; a brand new one.

Ross   Okay? Ready? Ready, Martin; here we go; just . . .
be yourself.

Martin   Really?

Ross (*a tiny bit testy*)   Well, no; maybe not. Put on your
public face.

Martin (*overly cheerful*)   Okay!

Ross   And don't switch in the middle.

Martin (*more*)   Okay!

Ross (*under his breath*)   Jesus! (*Announcer voice.*) Good evening.
This is Ross Tuttle. Welcome to 'People Who Matter'.
Some people have birthdays and no one pays them any
mind. Well . . . family, of course, friends. And others . . .
well, some people are . . . I was going to say special but
that's a . . . dumb word, for everyone matters, everyone's
special. But some people matter in extraordinary ways, in
ways which affect the lives of the rest of us – enrich them,
inform them. Some people, I guess, are, well . . . more
extraordinary than others. Martin Gray – whom you've met
on this programme before – is such a man, such a person.
Good evening, Martin.

Martin   Good . . . uh, evening, Ross. (*Sotto voce.*) It's mid-
afternoon.

Ross (*quiet snarl*)   I know. Shut up! (*Announcer voice.*) Three
things happened to you this week, Martin. You became the
youngest person ever to win the Pritzker Prize,

architecture's version of the Nobel. Also this week you were chosen to design the World City, the twenty-seven billion dollar dream city of the future, financed by US electronics technology and set to rise in the wheatfields of our middle west. Also, this week, you celebrated your fiftieth birthday. Happy birthday, Martin, and congratulations!

Martin (*brief pause; casual*)   Thanks, Ross.

Ross   Quite a week, Martin!

Martin (*a little puzzled*)   Yes; yes it was. Quite a week.

Ross (*big*)   How does it feel, Martin?

Martin   Becoming fifty?

Ross (*pushing*)   No. *All* of it. Yes.

Martin   Well . . .

Ross (*sensing no answer is coming*)   It must be amazing! No, thrilling!

Martin   Turning fifty? No: not really.

Ross   (*not amused*)   No! The other! The World City! The Pritzker! All that!

Martin (*genuine surprise*)   Oh, that! Well, yes . . . amazing, thrilling.

Ross (*prompting*)   For one so young.

Martin (*innocent*)   Fifty is young?

Ross (*controlling himself*)   For the Pritzker Prize! Where were you when they told you?

Martin   I was at the gym; I'd taken all my clothes off, and Stevie called me there.

Ross   Stevie is your wife.

Martin   I know that.

Ross   How did it make you feel?

Martin   Stevie being my wife?

Ross   No: the prize.

Martin   Well, it was . . . gratifying – not being naked, but . . . hearing about it – the prize.

Ross (*exuberant*)   Weren't you . . . thunderstruck?!

Martin   Well, no; they'd hinted at it – the prize, I mean, and . . .

Ross (*heavily prompting*)   But it was pretty wonderful, wasn't it?

Martin (*understanding what to say*)   Yes; yes it was pretty wonderful – *is* pretty wonderful.

Ross   Tell us about The World City.

Martin   Well, you just *did*: twenty-seven billion dollars, and all, the wheatfields of Kansas, or whatever . . .

Ross   What an honour! What a duo of honours! You're at the . . . pinnacle of your success, Martin . . .

Martin (*considers that*)   You mean it's all downhill from here?

Ross   CUT! CUT! (*Camera down. To* **Martin**.) What's the matter with you?!

Martin   Sorry?

Ross   I can't shoot that! You were a million miles away!

Martin   (*considering*)   That far.

Ross   You want to try again?

Martin   Try what?

Ross   The taping! The programme!

Martin (*as if seeing the camera for the first time*)   Oooooh.

Ross   We're taping!

Martin (*unhappy*)   Yes; I know.

Ross (*nicely concerned*)   Something the matter?

Martin   I think so. Yes; probably.

Ross   Do you want to talk about it, as they say?

Martin   About what?

Ross   About what's the matter.

Martin (*concerned*)   Why? What's the matter?

Ross   You said something was the matter, that you think something's the matter.

Martin (*far away*)   Oh.

Ross   Forty years, Martin; we've known each other forty years – since we were ten.

Martin (*trying to understand*)   Yes. That gives you something? Rights, or something?

Ross   I'm your oldest friend.

Martin   No; my aesthetics professor at college; I still see him; he's a lot older than you; he's over ninety.

Ross (*so patient*)   Your longest friend: the person you've known the longest.

Martin   No; my Aunt Sarah; she's known me . . .

Ross (*trying to stay patient*)   She's not a friend!

Martin (*deep, quiet surprise*)   Oh?

Ross (*close to giving up*)   No; she's a relative; relatives are not friends!

Martin   Oh, now . . .

Ross   Are not the same as friends. Jesus!

Martin Aha! Yes; well, you're right. I've known you longer as a friend than anyone. (*Tiny pause.*) Why is that relevant?

Ross Because you're troubled, and I thought that as your oldest friend I might be able to . . .

Martin I am? Is that true?

Ross You said that something was the matter!

Martin (*not remembering*) I did, hunh?

Ross Why are you so . . . ? (*Can't find the word.*)

Martin Are you still shooting? Are you still on?

Ross (*heavy sigh*) No. We'll try to do it at the studio later. Sorry.

Martin Can I get up now?

Ross If you want to; if you're not happy.

Martin Why are you talking to me like I was a child?

Ross Because you're acting like one.

Martin (*innocent*) I am?

Ross Probably the most important week of your life . . .

Martin (*impressed, if uninvolved*) Really!

Ross . . . and you act like you don't know whether you're coming or going, like you don't know where you are.

Martin (*self-absorbed, almost to himself*) Maybe it's . . . love or something.

Ross Maybe what is?

Martin Like a child.

Ross (*bingo!*) You're having an affair!

Martin SHHHHHHHH! I mean, Jesus!

Ross (*shrugs*) It's okay; he's not having an affair.

Martin   Jesus! Too bad you didn't bring the crew; they'd love this.

Ross (*cool*)   They know their business.

Martin   And . . . ?

Ross   And . . . ?

Martin   Aren't you guys friendly any more?

Ross   They know their business. What do you want me to do – have them over for *dinner*? Have every crew over for dinner?

Martin (*puzzled*)   No, I guess not. (*Afterthought.*) Why *not?*

Ross   Hm?

Martin   Why *not* have them over for dinner?

Ross   Oh, for God's sake, Martin!

Martin (*hands up, defensively*)   Okay! Okay! Jesus!

Ross   It's just that . . . it's just that I don't . . . mix with . . .

Martin (*joyful*)   The *help*?! You don't mix with the *help*?!

Ross   What *is* wrong with you today?! That's not what I meant, and you *know* it.

Martin (*half-serious, half-joking*)   You're a snob! I guess I've always known that. For all your left-wing, proletarian background you're a *snob*: worst kind.

Ross (*a plea; a warning*)   We're best friends, remember?

Martin   Meaning . . . ?

Ross   We like each other.

Martin (*'so, that's it!'*)   Ohhhhhhhh!

Ross   More than anyone.

Martin (*ibid.*)   Ohhhhh! (*Considers it.*) Right; yes. Who else can I be cranky with?

Ross   Stevie?

Martin   Ya know, Stevie doesn't take too well to cranky any more. If she's developed a flaw, it's that. 'Don't be so cranky, Martin.'

Ross   Pity.

They've gentled down now.

Martin (*shrugs*)   Well . . . *you* know.

Ross (*pause*)   So you're in love.

Martin   With Stevie? Sure! Twenty-two years now.

Ross   No, I mean . . . 'in love'. Ficky-fack! Humpty-doodle!

Martin   What on earth are you talking about?! 'Humpty-doodle'?!

Ross   You said you were in love – outside of Stevie, as I read it.

Martin (*genuine*)   Really? I don't remember.

Ross (*impatient sigh; abrupt*)   O . . . kay! That does it!

Martin (*as* **Ross** *gathers up stuff; true innocence*)   Where are you going?

Ross (*staring him down*)   I'm gathering my things and I'm taking my left-wing . . . what was it?

Martin   Uh . . . proletarian.

Ross   . . . proletarian self outa here.

Martin   'But, why!' as the . . .

Ross   Look, I came here to fucking interview you.

Martin   Fine.

Ross   To boost your ego even more than . . .

Martin   I have no ego.

Ross   Bullshit! Even more than where it is already and you fuck that up.

Martin   Fine. You say fuck a lot.

Ross   You say fine a lot. (*He laughs; so does* **Martin**.)

Martin   Words beginning with F.

Ross (*smiles*)   Yeah. (*Pause.*) So; tell me about it.

Martin (*shy*)   About . . . ?

Ross (*gently urging*)   Your new love.

Martin   Oh; that.

Ross   Yes.

Martin   I don't know that I want to . . .

Ross   Yes; you do.

Martin   . . . that I can.

Ross   Try.

Martin (*small smile*)   You're persistent.

Ross   Best friend. (**Martin** *tries to talk; can't.*) Best friend.

Martin (*frustrated explosion*)   Okay! Okay! (*Heavy, slow sigh, long pause.*) I don't know if I ever thought that . . . well, that Stevie and I would be . . . well, no; we're not. (*Pause.*)

Ross   Are you telling me about it?

Martin   I'm starting to . . . or maybe I'm beginning to start.

Ross   Oh; okay.

Martin   As I said, it never occurred to me that anything like this would come up. 'Cause we've always been good together – good in bed, good out; always honest, always . . . considerate. I've not been unfaithful our whole marriage – I want you to know this – never physically untrue, as they say.

Ross   That's amazing. It's wonderful, but . . . wow!

Martin   Yes: wow. Oh, I've been groped in the kitchen by a cutie or two, late, a party, once or twice, and I've had my hand a couple of places a couple of times, but I've never . . . *done* anything. You follow.

Ross   Yes; I follow.

Martin   It never seemed . . . well, necessary, either to be able to do a comparison, or . . . even for its own sake. I never needed it, I guess. Do you remember that time, that college reunion weekend you and I decided to call that service they'd told us about . . . the gang had told us about?

Ross (*rueful laugh*)   The Ladies Aid Society?

Martin   Yeah, and you called them, and . . .

Ross   . . . and we had a couple of bimbos over . . .

Martin   Bimbi.

Ross   Yes? (*Broad.*) Ohhhhh, I remember.

Martin   . . . And you were married already, and Stevie and I were dating . . . or going together . . .

Ross   . . . or whatever.

Martin   Yes.

Ross (*trying to recall*)   What were their names?

Martin   Mine was Alice.

Ross   Big girl.

Martin   Large Alice.

Ross   Right! Mine was Trudy, or Trixie, or . . .

Martin   April.

Ross   Yes? April?

Martin   Yes; April.

Ross (*interior*)   Oh, shit; April's called April.

Martin (*registering it*)   Yes; she is.

Ross   Shit. (*Pause; recovers.*)   And we had them up to our room – two beds, two hookers.

Martin   Just like when we roomed together.

Ross   A kind of reunion for the reunion.

Martin   Yes, I guess so. And do you remember what happened?

Ross   I don't know. What happened?

Martin   I couldn't do it? Couldn't perform?

Ross (*recalls*)   Oh, yeah. You'd never had that problem when we were undergrads! I'd be pumping away, you pumping away in the next bed.

Martin   I hadn't met Stevie.

Ross (*soberer*)   Right.

Martin   That night at the reunion with large Alice . . .

Ross   You were going with Stevie . . .

Martin   Right.

Ross   I remember.

Martin   I don't know why I ever thought I wanted to . . . *you* know.

Ross   No. Right.

Martin   I was already in love with Stevie and I didn't know how much.

Ross (*a little deriding*)   Amazing theory: the heart rules the dick. I always thought that the dick was driven by . . .

Martin   Don't be cynical.

Ross   Oh, a new part of my left-wing . . . what?

Martin   Proletarian.

Ross   Yes. My left-wing, proletarian, snobbish *cynical* self.

Martin   Right, and not new. (*They both smile.*) You *do* see, don't you? In love with Stevie, she owns every part of me. Look, when I'm travelling, and Stevie's *here*, and I get itchy . . .

Ross   You give yourself a handjob and you think about Stevie – about you and Stevie.

Martin (*shy*)   Yes.

Ross (*shakes his head; noncommittal*)   Wonderful.

Martin   I didn't catch your tone.

Ross   There wasn't any. Go on; how did you fuck it up?

Martin (*truly confused*)   What? Fuck *what* up?

Ross   Are you playing games?

Martin   No. Fuck *what* up?

Ross (*serious*)   Your life, apparently – you and Stevie. How'd you fuck it up?

Martin (*pause*)   Oh. (*Pause.*) That.

Ross (*impatient*)   Getting an answer out of you . . .

Martin   Okay! Okay! As I told you, I've never been unfaithful, never needed it . . . never . . .

Ross   Yeah, yeah; right. You told me.

Martin   And then . . . one day . . . (*Stops.*)

Ross (*after a silence*)   Yeah?!

Martin   And then one day. (*Says nothing more.*)

Ross (*long pause*)   That's it?!

Martin (*goes ahead*)   And then one day . . . one day . . . well, I was house-hunting – barn-hunting, actually. Stevie and I had decided it was time to have a real country place –

a farm, maybe – we deserved it. So, I was in the car about sixty miles out from the city. Stevie couldn't come with me.

Ross   Beyond the suburbs.

Martin   Yes; beyond the suburbs. Farms around it, small farms. And I found a wonderful place, a wonderful old farmhouse, and a lot of land.

Ross   The old back twenty, or whatever it is.

Martin   Right! Whatever. And I called Stevie, and told her she had to see it, and I'd put a hold on it till she could see it. And Stevie was . . . well, 'A farm?' she said, but I said 'Wait!' and the real estate guy was okay with that for a while. And I was driving out of the town back to the highway, and I stopped at the top of a hill.

Ross   Crest.

Martin   Right. And I stopped, and the view was . . . well, not spectacular, but . . . wonderful. Fall, you know? With leaves turning and the town below me and great scudding clouds and those country smells.

Ross   Cow shit, and all that.

Martin (*broad country parody*)   New mown hay, fella! The smell a country; the smell a apples! (*Normal tone again.*) The roadside stands, with corn and other stuff piled high, and baskets full of other thing – beans and tomatoes and those great white peaches you only get late summer . . .

Ross (*broad*)   The whole thing; right.

Martin (*shakes his head*)   Oh, you city boys! And from up there I could trace the roads out towards the farm, and it gave me a kind of shiver.

Ross   The ludicrous often does.

Martin   Anyway . . .

Ross   Anyway.

Martin   Anyway, it was pretty wonderful. And I was getting back in the car, about to get back in the car, all my loot – vegetables and stuff . . . (*Change of tone to quiet wonder.*) and it was then that I saw her. (*Sees it.*) Just . . . just looking at me.

Ross   Daisy Mae! Blonde hair to her shoulders, big tits in the calico blouse, bare midriff, blonde down at the navel, piece a straw in her teeth . . .

Martin (*gentle admonishing smile*)   You don't understand.

Ross   No? No blonde hair? No tits?

Martin   No. And there she was, looking at me with those eyes.

Ross   And it was love.

Martin   You don't understand.

Ross   No? It *wasn't* love?

Martin   No. Yes; yes, it was love, but I didn't know it right then. (*To himself.*) How could I?

Ross   Right then, it was good old lust, eh? Dick starting to get big in your pants . . .

Martin (*sad*)   You *don't* understand. (*Pause.*) I didn't know *what* it was – what I was feeling. It was . . . it wasn't like anything I'd felt before; it was . . . so . . . amazing, so . . . extraordinary! There she was, just looking at me, with those *eyes* of hers, and . . .

Ross (*impatient*)   Well, did you *talk* to her?

Martin (*incredulous laugh*)   Did I *what*?!

Ross   Did you *talk* to her?!

Martin (*considers it*)   Hunh! Yes; yes, I did. I went up to her, to where she was, and I spoke to her, and she came towards me and . . . and those eyes, and I touched her face, and . . . (*Abrupt.*) I don't want to talk about it; I can't *talk* about it.

Ross   All right; let me help you. You're *seeing* her.

Martin (*sad laugh*)   Yes; oh, yes; I'm *seeing* her.

Ross   You're having an affair with her.

Martin (*confused*)   A what? Having a *what*?!

Ross (*hard*)   You're *screwing* her.

Martin (*sudden vision of it*)   Yes; yes; I'm *screwing* her. Oh, Jesus!

Ross (*softer*)   And you're in love

Martin   That's it, you see.

Ross   What is? What do I see?

Martin   I *am* seeing her; I *am* having . . . an affair, I guess. No! That's not the right word. I am . . . (*Winces.*) screwing her, as you put it – all of which is . . . beyond even . . . yes, I'm doing all that.

Ross (*prompting*)   . . . And you're in love with her.

Martin (*begins to cry*)   Yes! Yes! I am! I'm in love with her. Oh, Jesus! Oh, Sylvia! Oh, Sylvia!

Ross (*after a respectful pause*)   I almost dare not ask this, but . . . who is Sylvia?

Martin   I can't tell you!

Ross   Who else *but* me? You can't tell Stevie, it would . . .

Martin   NO!

Ross   Then, who is she? Who is Sylvia?

Martin *pauses; goes to his wallet, brings out a photo, looks at it, hesitates, then hands it to* **Ross**, *not looking as he does so.* **Ross** *takes the photo, looks at it, double-takes, begins a huge guffaw, which becomes a coughing.*

Martin (*shy*)   Don't laugh. Please; don't laugh.

Ross (*staring at photo; straightforward*)   This is Sylvia.

Martin (*nods*)   Yes.

Ross (*pinning it down*)   This is Sylvia . . . who you're fucking.

Martin (*winces*)   Don't say that. (*It just comes out.*) Whom.

Ross   . . . With whom you're having an affair.

Martin (*soft; nodding*)   Yes. (*Pause.*) Yes.

Ross   How long now?

Martin (*soft*)   Six months.

Ross   Jesus. You *have* to tell Stevie.

Martin   I can't! I couldn't do that!

Ross   You *have* to . . . and if you don't, I will.

Martin (*begging*)   No! Ross! Please!

Ross (*genuine*)   You're in very serious trouble.

Martin (*pause; little boy*)   I am?

Ross (*quiet; shaking his head as he looks at the photo*)   You sure are, buddy; you sure are.

Martin   But, Ross, you don't under . . .

Ross (*huge*)   THIS IS A GOAT! YOU'RE HAVING AN AFFAIR WITH A GOAT! YOU'RE FUCKING A GOAT!

Martin (*long pause; factual*)   Yes.

Scene Two

The living room; a day later. **Martin**, **Stevie** *and* **Billy**; **Stevie** *holding a letter.*

Billy (*to* **Martin**)   You're doing *what*?! You're fucking a *goat*?!

Martin (*indicating* **Stevie**, *who is at the window, facing out*) Billy! Please!

Billy   Jesus Christ!

Martin   Don't swear.

Billy (*scoffing laugh*)   Don't *what*?!

Martin   Don't swear; you're too young.

Billy (*considers a moment, then*)   FUCK THAT!

Martin   Billy! Your mother!

Billy (*scoffing laugh*)   You're fucking a fucking goat and you tell me not to *swear*?!

Martin   You know, your *own* sex life leaves a little to . . .

Stevie (*still at the window; ice*)   All right, you two!

Billy (*to* **Martin**)   At least what I do is with . . . persons!

Stevie (*turning into the room*)   I said, all right, you two!

Billy   Goat-fucker!

Martin   Fucking faggot!

Stevie   I said, all right!

A silence.

Billy (*to* **Martin**; *soft, hurt*)   Fucking faggot? You called me a fucking *faggot*?!

Martin (*gentle; to* **Billy**)   I'm . . . I'm sorry.

Stevie (*even*)   Your father's sorry, Billy.

Martin   I'm sorry. (*To get rid of the whole subject.*) You're gay, and that's fine, and I don't give a shit what you put where. (*Thinks about it.*) I don't care one way or the other is what I mean.

Billy   Yeah! Sure!

Stevie (*cool*)   I said your father's sorry for calling you a fucking faggot because he's not that kind of man. He's a decent, liberal, right-thinking, talented, famous, gentle man (*Hard*) who right now would appear to be fucking a goat; and *I* would like to talk about *that, if* you don't mind. *Or* . . . even if you *do.*

Billy (*nice*)   Sure, Mom; I'm sorry; you go right ahead.

Martin (*sighs*)   Oh, dear.

Stevie (*objective*)   Let's review Ross's letter, shall we? (*Waves it.*)

Martin (*hurt and enraged*)   How *could* he?! How could he do such a thing?!

Stevie (*ice*)   How could he – best friend to both of us, a man you would trust with your wife – no? . . .

Martin   . . . Sure; sure . . .

Stevie   How could Ross write me this letter? (*Waves it again.*)

Martin   YES!

Stevie (*composed; cool; quoting*)   '. . . because I love you, Stevie, as much as I love Martin, because I love you both – respect you, love you – I can't stay silent at a time of crisis for you both, for Martin's public image, and your own deeply devoted . . . '

Martin   BULLSHIT!

Stevie   Yes?

Martin   Yes!

Stevie   So; anyhow; let's not pretend he never wrote the
letter; let's not pretend I didn't get it in the mail today – nice
that: no electronic nonsense – and let us not pretend that I
did not read it.

Martin   No; no, of course not.

Stevie   And let us not pretend that Ross does not tell me
that you are having an affair with . . . (*Looks.*) how does he
put it? . . . 'an affair with a certain Sylvia who, I am
mortified to tell you . . . ' He does get flowery, doesn't he!

Martin   Yes; yes, he does.

Stevie   'I am mortified to tell you is a goat.'

Billy   Jesus!

Stevie/Martin   Will you be still!?!

Billy (*dramatically cowering*)   Hey! Sure! Jesus!

Stevie (*back to business; quoting again*)   'You will, of course, be
shocked and greatly distressed . . . ' No kidding! Uh . . .
'shocked and greatly distressed to know of this, but I felt it
my obligation to be the one to bear these tidings . . . '

Martin (*some disbelief*)   Tidings?

Stevie   Yes; 'tidings'.

Martin   Jesus! Of comfort and joy?

Stevie   ' . . . as I'm sure you'd rather hear it all from a
dear friend . . . ' As opposed to *what*?! The RSPCA?!

Martin (*woe*)   Oh, God; oh, God.

Stevie   'Doubtless, Martin . . . ' Doubtless?

Martin   Probably.

Stevie   ' . . . Doubtless, Martin will tell you all I have not,
all I cannot.' (*To* **Martin**.) What are friends for, eh?

Billy (*really sad*)   Oh, Dad!

Martin   Poor Dad?

Billy   What?

Martin   Nothing.

Stevie (*level*)   So, now you will tell me all that Ross has not, cannot. After you tell me what friends are for, of course.

Martin   Oh . . . Stevie . . . (*Starts to move to her.*)

Stevie (*abrupt; cold*)   Stay away from me; stay there. You smell of goat, you smell of shit, you smell of all I cannot imagine being able to smell. Stay *away* from me!

Martin (*arms wide; hopeless*)   I *love* you!

Billy (*softly*)   Jesus.

Stevie   You *love* me. Let's see if I understand the phrase. You *love* me.

Martin   Yes!

Stevie   But I'm a human being; I have only two breasts; I walk upright; I give milk only on special occasions; I use the toilet. (*Begins to cry.*) You love me? I don't understand.

Martin (*more hopeless*)   Oh, God!

Stevie   How can you love me when you love so much less?

Martin (*even more hopeless*)   Oh, God.

Billy   Fucking a goat?!

Martin (*to* **Billy***; sharp*)   That does it! Out!

Billy (*To* **Stevie***; arms wide*)   What did I *say*? I said he was . . .

Martin   Enough!

Billy   For Christ's sake, I . . .

Martin   Go to your room!

Stevie (*almost laughing*)   Oh, really, Martin!

Billy (*incredulous*)   Go to my room?!

Martin   Go to your *room*!

Billy   What am I – eight, or something? Go to my *room*?

Stevie   You'd better go, Billy. If you stay you might learn something.

Martin (*to* **Stevie**)   Nicely put.

Stevie (*coldly*)   Thanks.

Billy (*to* **Stevie**)   You want me to leave you here with this . . . this . . . *pervert*?!

Stevie (*to help*)   Just go to your room, Billy, or go outside, or . . .

Martin   . . . or go to one of your public urinals, or one of those death clubs, or . . .

Billy   KNOCK IT OFF!

Martin (*impressed*)   Wow!

Billy (*sneering*)   You seem to know a lot about all that.

Martin (*not defensive*)   I *read*.

Billy   Sure. (*To* **Stevie**.) I'll go if you think it's okay, Ma; I'll go. (*To* **Martin**.) But not to your . . . 'places'. I will probably go to my room, and I'll probably close my door, and I'll probably lie down on my bed, and I'll probably start crying and it'll probably get louder and worse, but you probably won't hear it – either of you – because you'll be too busy killing each other. But I'll be there and my little eight-year-old heart will for certain be breaking – in twain, as they say.

Martin (*some awe; no contempt*)   Very good; very good.

Stevie (*preoccupied*)   Yes; very good, Billy.

Billy (*fleeing; near tears*)   Jesus Christ!

Stevie (*as he exits*)   Billy . . .

Martin (*quietly*)   Let him go. (*Silence; quietly.*) Well, now; just you and me.

Stevie (*pause*)   Yes.

Martin (*pause*)   I take it you want to talk about it?

Stevie (*awful chuckle*)   Oh, God! (*Afterthought.*) You *take* it?

Martin   Is that a 'yes'?

Stevie (*cold; precise*)   I was out shopping today – dress gloves, if you want to know. I still wear them – for weddings and things . . .

Martin (*puzzled*)   Who's getting married?

Stevie (*huge*)   SHUT UP!

Martin (*winces*)   Sorry.

Stevie (*normal tone again*)   . . . dress gloves, and then to the fish people for shad roe – it's just come in – and then back home, and you were gone and I heard Billy's music up in his room and there was the mail. You'd gone out before it came – not that it would have mattered: we don't read each others'.

Martin   Would that we did.

Stevie   Oh? I would have found out sooner or later. And there was Ross's letter. 'Ross? Writing to me? Whatever for?!'

Martin (*softly*)   Oh, God.

Stevie   . . . And I was standing in the pantry. I'd put the roe away and had left the kitchen and was moving to the dining room on my way to the stairs when I began to read it.

Martin   Ross shouldn't have done this. He *knows* he shouldn't have done . . .

Stevie (*Reading; steady, almost amused*)   'Dearest Stevie . . . '

Martin   Oh, God.

Stevie   'This is the hardest letter I've ever had to write.'

Martin   Sure!

Stevie   You doubt it? '. . . the hardest letter I've ever had to write, and to my dearest friends. But because I love you, Stevie, as much as I love Martin, because I love you both – respect you, love you – I can't stay silent at a time of crisis for you both, for Martin's public image and your own deeply devoted . . . '

Martin   As I said, bullshit.

Stevie   . . . 'self. I must put it baldly, for hinting would only put off the inevitable. Martin – and he told me this himself' . . . (*Aside.*) I would have liked to have been listening to *that* conversation!

Martin   No you wouldn't.

Stevie (*reading again*)   'Martin is having an affair with a certain Sylvia . . . ' (*To* **Martin**.) Oh, God, I thought; at least it's someone I don't know; at least it's not Ross's first wife, the one I thought you might if you were going to . . .

Martin (*surprise*)   Rebecca?

Stevie   Yes, or maybe your new assistant . . .

Martin (*bewildered*)   Who? Ted Ryan?

Stevie   No; the *other* one – the one with the hooters.

Martin   Oh; Lucy something.

Stevie   Yes: Lucy 'something'. You men are the end. Where was I? (*Reads again.*) . . . 'an affair with a certain Sylvia who, I am mortified to tell you . . . is a goat. You will, of course, be shocked and greatly disturbed to know of this, but I felt it my obligation to be the one to bear these tidings, as I'm sure you'd rather hear it from a dear friend. Doubtless, Martin . . .' Doubtless?

Martin (*shrugs*)   Sounds right.

Stevie   'Doubtless, Martin will tell you all I have not . . .
all I cannot. With profound affection for you both, Ross.'
(*Pause*.) Well.

Martin   Yes. 'Well.'

Stevie (*not eager; dogged*)   We will now discuss it.

Martin (*heavy sigh*)   Of course, though you won't
understand.

Stevie   Oh? Do you know what I thought – what I
thought after I'd read the letter, right to the end?

Martin   No, I don't want to know . . . or guess.

Stevie   Well, I laughed, of course: a grim joke but an
awfully funny one. 'That Ross, I tell you, that Ross! You go
too far, Ross. It's funny . . . in its . . . awful way, but it's way
overboard, Ross!' So, I shook my head and laughed – at the
awfulness of it, the absurdity, the awfulness; some things are
so awful you have to laugh – and then I listened to myself
laughing, and I began to wonder why I *was* – *laughing*. 'It's
not funny when you come right down to it, Ross.' Why *was* I
laughing? And just like that (*Snaps her fingers*.) I stopped; I
stopped laughing. I realised – probably in the way if you
suddenly fell off a building – 'oh, shit! I've fallen off a
building and I'm going to die; I'm going to go splat on the
sidewalk'; like *that* – that it wasn't a joke at all; it was awful
and absurd, but it wasn't a joke. And everything tied in –
Ross coming here to interview you yesterday, the funny
smell, the Noël Coward bit we did about you having an
affair, and with a goat. You said it right out and I laughed.
You *told* me! You came right out and fucking *told* me, and I
laughed, and I made jokes about going to the feed store and
I *laughed*. I fucking laughed! Until it stopped; until the
laughter stopped. Until it all came together – Ross's letter
and all the rest: that odd smell . . . the mistress's perfume on
you. And so I knew.

Martin   Stevie, I'm so . . .

Stevie (*rather sad*)   Shut up. And so I knew. And next, of course, came believing it. Knowing it – knowing it's true is one thing, but *believing* what you *know* . . . well, there's the tough part. We all prepare for jolts along the way, disturbances of the peace, the lies, the evasions, the infidelities – *if* they happen. (*Very off-hand.*) I've never had an affair, by the way, all our years together; not even with a cat, or . . . *any*thing.

Martin   Oh, Stevie . . .

Stevie   We prepare for . . . things, for lessenings, even; inevitable . . . lessenings, and we think we can handle everything, whatever comes along, but we don't know, *do* we! (*Right at* **Martin**.) *Do* we!

Martin (*bereaved*)   No; no, we don't.

Stevie   Fucking *right* we don't! (*Didactic.*) Something can happen that's outside the rules, that doesn't relate to The Way The Game Is Played. Death before you're ready to even think about it – that's part of the game. A stroke that leaves you sitting looking at an eggplant that the week before had been your husband – that's another. Emotional disengagement, gradual, so gradual you don't know it's happening, or sudden – not very often, but occasionally – that's another. You've read about spouses – God! I hate that word! – 'spouses' who all of a sudden start wearing dresses – yours, or their own collection – wives gone dyke . . . but if there's one thing you *don't* put on your plate, no matter how exotic your tastes may be, is . . . beastiality.

Martin   Don't! You don't understand.

Stevie   The fucking of animals! No, that's one thing you haven't thought about, one thing you've overlooked as a byway on the road of life, as the old soap has it. 'Well, I wonder when he'll start cruising livestock. I must ask Mother whether Dad did it and how *she* handled it.' No, that's the one thing you haven't thought about – nor could you conceive of. (*Pause; grimly cheerful.*) So! How was *your* day?

Martin (*pause; attempting the casual*)   Well . . . I had a good day at the office. Made the design for the World City even larger than . . .

Stevie (*fixed smile*)   Oh, good!

Martin   . . . and then I stopped by the haberdasher . . .

Stevie (*pretending to puzzle*)   Ha-ber-dash-er. That's someone who makes haberdash?

Martin   Haber, I think. Dash is part of doing it.

Stevie   Ah! *Then* what?

Martin   Hm? Well, then I drove back home, and . . .

Stevie   What! You didn't stop by to see your ladyfriend? Get a lick in?

Martin   She's in the country. Please, Stevie . . . *don't*!

Stevie (*feigned wonder*)   She's in the *country*!

Martin   I keep her there.

Stevie   Where?!

Martin   Please! Don't!

Stevie   Martin, did you ever think you'd come back from your splendid life, walk into your living room and find you had no life left?

Martin   Not specifically; no. (*Looks down.*)

Stevie   I think we'd better talk about this. If I'm going to kill you I need to know exactly why – all the details.

Martin (*shy*)   You really want to?

Stevie   What? Kill you?

Martin   No; learn about it.

Stevie (*big*)   No! I *don't* really want to! (*Normal tone again.*) I want the whole day to rewind – start over. I want the reel to reverse: to see the mail on the hall table where Billy's left it, then *not* see it because I haven't opened the door yet – not having gotten the dish yet because I haven't bought the gloves yet because I haven't left the house yet because I haven't gotten out of our bed because I haven't *waked* UP YET! (*Quieter.*) But . . . since I can't reverse time . . . yes, I *do* want to know. I'm reeling with it. (*Pleading.*) Make me not *believe* it! Please, make me *not believe* it.

Martin (*pause*) Why aren't you crying?

Stevie Because this is too serious. Do goats cry, by the way?

Martin I . . . I don't know. I haven't . . .

Stevie . . . made her cry yet?! What's the *matter* with you?!

Martin (*begging*) Stevie . . .

Stevie (*as if to someone else*) He can't even make a *goat* cry. What *good* is he? His son's probably weeping as we speak. That was pretty awful what you said to him, Martin, pretty awful. His son's probably lying on his bed, tears flowing; his wife *would* be crying (*harder*) except she can't be that weak right now. And you can't even make a goat cry?! Jeez!

Martin (*dogmatic*) I didn't say I *couldn't*; I said I *haven't*.

Stevie Well, the goats of this world must be very happy. Oh, you kid!

Martin (*starting to leave*) I can't *have* this conversation. I can't listen to you when you're . . .

Stevie (*blocking him*) You *stay* where you *are*! You will *have* this conversation, and with *me* and right *now*!

Martin (*retreating; sighing*) Where shall I start?

Stevie (*a threat*) Right at the beginning! (*Afterthought.*) Why do you call her Sylvia, by the way? Did she have a tag, or something? Or, was it more:

'Who is Sylvia,
   What is she
   That all our Goats commend her . . .'

Martin (*trying to be rational*)   No, it just seemed right. Very good, by the way.

Stevie   Thank you. You saw this . . . *thing* . . . this goat, and you said to yourself, 'This is Sylvia.' Or did you talk to it: 'Hello, Sylvia.' How the hell did you know it was a she – was a female? Bag of nipples dragging in the dung? Or, isn't this your first?!

Martin (*very quiet*)   She is my first; she is my only. But you don't understand. You . . .

Stevie (*contemptuous*)   Awww; I'm trying not to throw up.

Martin   Well, if that's the way you . . .

Stevie   *No*! Tell me.

Martin (*sighs*)   All right. As I said to Ross . . .

Stevie (*broad parody*)   'As I said to Ross . . . ' NO! Not 'As I said to Ross.' To *me*! As you say to *me*!

Martin (*annoyed*)   In any event . . .

Stevie   Not 'in any event!' No! *This* event!

Martin (*won't let it go*)   As I said to Ross . . .

Stevie (*impatient acquiescence*)   *Very* well; as you said to Ross.

Martin   Thank you. As I said to Ross, I'd gone to the country . . . to find the place we wanted, our . . . country *place*.

Stevie (*fact*)   You went out a lot.

Martin   Well, if you're after Utopia . . . (*Shrugs.*)

Stevie   Sure.

Martin   . . . unless you're one of those people finds it right off: 'That's it; that's the place.' Unless you're one of those you've got to nose around.

Stevie   Is that an ugly phrase? – 'nose around'?

Martin (*not too certain*)   I don't think so. Search. Is that better? (**Stevie** *shrugs*.) Search; look around. Close enough in to make it practical for our country needs. No more than an hour or so from . . .

Stevie (*scoffing*)   Our 'country needs'?

Martin   *You're* the one who said it. Verdancy: flowers and green leaves against steel and stone. Okay?

Stevie (*shrugs*)   Okay. (*Angry.*) And it's lovely. Now get to the *goat*!

Martin   I'm *getting* there. I'm *getting* to her.

Stevie   Stop calling it *her*!

Martin (*defending*)   *That* is what she *is*! It is a *she*! *She* is a *she*!

Stevie (*pathetic sneer*)   I suppose I should be grateful it wasn't a *male*, *isn't* a male goat.

Martin   Funny you should ask – as they say. There was a place I went to . . .

Stevie   Oh?

Martin   Well, when I realised something was wrong. I mean, when I realised people would *think* something was wrong, that what I was doing wasn't . . .

Stevie (*dispassionate*)   I *am* going to kill you.

Martin (*preoccupied*)   Yes; probably. It was a therapy place, a place people went to . . . to talk about it, about what they were doing . . . and with whom.

Stevie   *What*! Not *whom*! *What*! With *what*!

Martin (*sharp*). Whatever! A place! Please! Let me finish this! (**Stevie** *is silent.*) A place to talk about it; like AA, like Alcoholics Anonymous.

Stevie (*sneers*)   Goat-Fuckers Anonymous?

Martin (*oddly shocked*)   Please! (**Stevie** *hoots. Quieter.*) Please?

Stevie   Sorry. Destroy me.

Martin   It had no cute name; no AA; no . . . no nothing. Just . . . a place.

Stevie   How did you find it?

Martin   On-line.

Stevie (*toneless*)   Of course.

Martin   I went there . . . and there were – what? – ten of us . . . a group leader, or course.

Stevie   What was *he* fucking? *Who*; sorry.

Martin   He was cured, he said – odd phrase. Was off it.

Stevie (*very calm*)   Very well. What *had* he been fucking?

Martin (*matter-of-fact*)   A pig. A young pig.

Stevie *rises, finds a big ceramic table plate, smashes it, resits, or whatever.*

Stevie (*without emotion*)   Go on.

Martin (*indicates*)   Is there going to be a lot of that?

Stevie   Probably.

Martin   You don't want Billy down here; some things . . .

Stevie (*steaming*)   Some things are . . . *what*?! Private? Sacred? Husband telling wifey about a very peculiar therapy session? A *pig*?!

Martin (*a little embarassed*)   A small one, he said.

Stevie   Jesus!

Billy *rushes in from the hall.*

Billy   You two okay?

Martin   Yes-we're-fine-go-away-Billy.

Billy   Who's throwing things?

Stevie   I am; your mother is throwing things.

Billy   Is there going to be more?

Stevie   I imagine so.

Billy *(retrieving a small vase)*   I gave you this one; I think I'll take it upstairs.

Stevie *(as **Billy** turns to go)*   I would have noticed, Billy.

Billy *(shaking his head)*   Sure. You guys hold it down. *(Exits.)*

Stevie *(after him)*   I *would* have. *(Uncertain.)* I *think* I would have.

Martin *(pause)*   So, anyway; it was this place.

Stevie *(reconcentrating)*   A pig? Really?

Martin   Well, everyone had . . . *you* know . . .

Stevie   . . . some*one*, or some*thing*.

Martin   Yes.

Stevie *(light bulb)*   And was Clarissa Atherton there?

Martin   Who? Yes! That's where I got the card, and . . .

Stevie   And what is *she* fucking? *Who*?

Martin *(matter of fact)*   A dog, I think.

Stevie *finds a vase, crashes it to the floor.*

Stevie   A dog, you *think*.

Martin   Why would she lie? Why would anyone there lie?

Stevie   Damned if *I* know.

Martin (*sighs*)   And so I went there, and . . .

Stevie (*there is chaos behind the civility, of course*)   Did you all take your . . . friends with you – your pigs, your dogs, your goats, your . . .

Martin   No. We weren't there to talk about *them*; we were there about ourselves, our . . . our problems, as they called them.

Stevie   The livestock was all happy, you mean.

Martin   Well, no; there was this one . . . goose, I think it was . . . (**Stevie** *sweeps a bowl off a table.*) Shall we go outside?

Stevie (*hands on hips*)   Get *on* with it.

Martin (*so calm*)   All right; there was this one goose . . .

Stevie   *Not* geese! *Not* pigs! *Not* dogs! *Goats*! The subject is *goats*!

Martin   The subject is *a* goat; the subject is Sylvia. (*He sees* **Stevie** *looking for something to throw.*) No! Don't; please! Just listen! Sit and listen!

Stevie (*has a small bowl in her hands; sits*)   All right. I'm listening.

Martin   I said, most of the people there were having problems, were . . . ashamed, or – what is the word? – conflicted . . . were . . . needed to talk about it while . . . while I went there, I guess, to find out why they were all there.

Stevie (*as if the language were unfamiliar*) Pardon?

Martin   I didn't understand why they were there – why they were all so . . . unhappy; what was wrong with . . . with . . . being in love . . . like that. (**Stevie** *gently separates her hands, letting the bowl fall between her legs, break.*) There's so much I have to explain.

Stevie (*deep quiet irony*)   Oh?

Martin (*rises, moves a little away*)   You must promise to be still. Sit there and please listen, and then maybe when I've finished you . . . just listen; please.

Stevie (*sad smile*)   How could I not?

Martin   I went there . . . because I couldn't come to *you* with it.

Stevie   Oh?

Martin   Well . . . *think* about it.

Stevie (*does*)   I suppose you're right.

Martin   And most of them had a problem, had a long history. The man with the pig was a farmboy, and he and his brothers, when they were kids, just . . . *did* it . . . *naturally*; it was what they did . . . with the pigs. (*Knits brow.*) Or piglets, perhaps; that wasn't clear.

Stevie   Naturally; of course.

Martin   Are you agreeing?

Stevie   No. Just get on with it.

Martin   It was what they did. Maybe it was better than . . .

Stevie (*hoots with derision*)   . . . than with each other, or their sisters, or their grandmothers? You've got to be kidding!

Martin   No one got hurt.

Stevie   HUNH!

Martin   We'll talk about that.

Stevie   You *bet* we will!

Martin (*sighs*)   Most of them had a reason, the man with the pig more a matter of . . . habit than anything else, I guess . . . comfort, familiarity.

Stevie (*eyes heavenward*)   Jesus!

Martin   Though he was off it . . . 'cured', as he put it, which I found odd.

Stevie   Of course.

Martin   I mean . . . if he was happy . . .

Stevie *knocks over the small side table where she is sitting, never taking her eyes off* **Martin**.

Stevie (*ironic*)   Ooops!

Martin   When he was doing it, I mean. Must you? Though I suppose he wasn't . . . no longer was happy.

Stevie (*feigned surprise*)   You mean you didn't *ask* him?

Martin   No; no, I didn't. The lady with the German Shepherd . . .

Stevie   Clarissa?

Martin   No; another one. The lady with the Shepherd, it turned out she had been raped by her father *and* her brother when she was twelve, or so . . . continually raped, one watching the other, she told us . . .

Stevie   . . . and so she took up with a *dog*?!

Martin (*no opinion*)   Yes; it would seem. The man with the goose was . . . hideously ugly – I could barely look at him – and I suppose he thought he could never . . . *you* know.

Stevie (*cool*)   Do I?

Martin   Try and imagine.

Stevie (*calm; sad*)   I doubt I can.

Martin   *Try*: so ugly, no woman – no *man* – would even *think* of . . . 'doing it' with you – *ever*.

Stevie   One in the hand, et cetera. But . . . a goose?!

Martin (*sad smile*)   Not everyone is satisfied that way . . . one in the hand. No matter. And *I* was unhappy there, for *they* were all unhappy.

Stevie   My goodness.

Martin   And I didn't know why.

Stevie (*considers it*)   Really? I think we've hit upon why I'm going to kill you.

Martin (*onward*)   There's something else I want you to understand.

Stevie (*sarcasm*)   Oh? Something else?

Martin   It's something I told Ross.

Stevie   Not him again.

Martin   He *is* my best friend.

Stevie (*actressy*)   Oh? And I thought *I* was!

Martin (*undeterred; calm*)   I told him that in all our time together – yours and mine – all our marriage – I've never been unfaithful.

Stevie (*a beat; fake astonishment*)   *Hunh!*

Martin (*onward*)   Never in all our years. Oh, early on, one of your friends would grope me in the kitchen at a party, or . . .

Stevie   I love my friends; they have taste.

Martin   Never unfaithful; never once. I've never even wanted to. We're so good together, you and I.

Stevie   A perfect fit, eh?

Martin (*sincere*)   Yes!

Stevie   You'd never imagine that a marriage could be so perfect.

Martin   Yes! I mean *no*; I *hadn't*.

Stevie (*advertisement*)   Great sex, good cook, even does windows.

Martin   Be serious!

Stevie   No! It's too serious for that. (*Afterthought.*) Fuck you, by the way.

Martin   Never once! People looked at me, said 'What's the matter with you?! Don't you have any . . . you know, lust?' and 'Sure,' I said, 'I've got plenty. All for Stevie.'

Stevie (*shakes her head; sing-song*)   La-di-da; la-di-fuckin'-da!

Martin (*rage*)   Listen to me!

Stevie (*army drill*)   Yes, sir! (*Softer.*) Yes, sir.

Martin   All the men I knew were 'having affairs' . . . *see*ing other women, and laughing about it – at the club, on the train. I felt . . . well, I almost felt like a misfit. 'What's the matter with you, Martin?! You mean you're only doing it with your wife?! What kind of man *are* you?!'

Stevie   You men *must* be fun together.

Martin   Odd man out. I only wanted *you*.

Stevie (*pause; quietly*)   And *I* have something to tell *you*.

Martin (*anticipating, with dread*)   Oh, no! Don't tell me that you've been with . . .

Stevie (*hands up; shakes her head*)   Hush. In all our marriage I've never even wanted anyone but you.

Martin (*deeply sad*)   Oh, Stevie.

Stevie   My mother told me – we really *were* good friends; I'm sorry you never knew her.

Martin   I am, too.

Stevie   We talked together like sisters, by God; we talked the night away, two 'girls' talking; we were that good friends, but she sure knew how to be a 'parent' when she needed to, when she wanted to keep me very . . . level. And she said to me – I never told you this – 'Be sure you marry someone you're in love with – deeply and wholly in love with – but be careful who you fall in love with, because you might marry him.' (**Martin** *chuckles, quietly, ruefully.*) 'Your father and I have the best marriage anyone could possibly have,' she said to me, over and over. 'Be sure you do, too.'

Martin   Stevie, I . . .

Stevie   'Be careful who you marry,' she said to me. And I *was*. I *fell* in love with you? No . . . I rose into love with you and have – what – *cherished*? you, all these years, been proud of all you've done, been happy with our . . . funny son, been . . . well, happy. I guess that's the word. No, I don't guess; I *know*. (*Begins to cry.*) I've been happy. (*More.*) Look at me, Mother; I've married the man I loved (*More.*) and I've been . . . so . . . happy.

Martin (*moves to her; touches her*)   Oh, Stevie . . .

Stevie (*huge; swipes objects off the coffee table*) GET YOUR GOAT-FUCKING HANDS OFF ME! (*Retreats to the wall, arms wide, sobbing greatly.*)

Martin (*reacts as if he's touched a hot stove*)   All right! No more!

Stevie   Yes! *More*! Finish it! Vomit it all up! Puke it out all over me. I'll never be less ready. So . . . *do* it! DO IT! I've laid it all out for you; I'm naked on the table; take all your knives! Cut me! Scar me forever!

Martin (*thinks a moment*)   Before or *after* I vomit on you? (*Gently; hands up to appease.*) Sorry; sorry.

Stevie (*a shaking voice*)   Women in deep woe often mix their metaphors.

Martin (*pacifying*)   Yes; yes.

Stevie   Get *on* with it! (*Afterthought.*) Very good, by the way.

Martin (*rue*)   Thanks.

Stevie   And hopelessly inappropriate.

Martin   Yes; sorry.

Stevie (*casually overturns a chair*)   Get on with it, I said.

Martin   Are you going to do that with *all* the furniture?

Stevie (*looks around*)   I think so. You may have to help me with some of it.

Martin   Truce! Truce!

Stevie (*takes a painting, breaks it over something*) NO! NO TRUCE! *All* of it! Now!

Martin   That was my mother's painting.

Stevie   It still is! (*Prompting.*) You found us our lovely country place.

Martin (*girds*)   And the day I found it – I called you. You remember: I told you I'd put a hold on it.

Stevie   I'll never forget.

Martin   And I was driving out of the town, back to the highway, and I stopped at the top of a hill . . .

Stevie   Crest.

Martin   What?! Who *are* you?!

Stevie   You stopped at the crest of a hill – on it, actually.

Martin   Yes. And I stopped, and the view was . . . wonderful. Not spectacular, but wonderful – fall, the leaves turning . . .

Stevie (*staring at him*)   A regular bucolic.

Martin   Yes; a regular bucolic. I stopped and got us things – vegetables and things. *You* remember.

Stevie (*denial*)   No; I don't.

Martin (*realising, going on*)   No matter. And it was then that I saw her.

Stevie (*grotesque incomprehension*)   *Who*?!

Martin (*deeply sad*)   Oh, Stevie . . .

Stevie (*heavy irony*)   *Who*?! *Who* could you have seen?!

Martin (*dogged*)   I'm going on with this. You asked. I'm going to get it all out.

Stevie (*eyes hard on him*)   Serves *me* right, I guess.

Martin   And I closed the trunk of the car, with all that I'd gotten – (*Pause.*) . . . and it was then that I saw her. And she was looking at me with . . . with those eyes.

Stevie (*staring at him*)   Oh, those eyes! (*Afterthought.*) *THEM* eyes!

Martin (*slow, deliberate*)   And what I felt was . . . it was unlike anything I'd ever felt before. It was so . . . amazing. There she was.

Stevie (*grotesque enthusiasm*)   Who?! Who?!

Martin   Don't. She was looking at me with those eyes of hers and . . . I melted, I think. I think that's what I did: I melted.

Stevie (*hideous enthusiasm*)   You melted!

Martin (*waves her off*)   I'd never seen such an expression. It was pure . . . and trusting and . . . and innocent; so . . . guileless.

Stevie (*sardonic echo*)   Guileless; innocent; pure. You've never seen children, or anything? You never saw Billy when he was a kid?

Martin (*pleading*)   Of course I did. Don't *mock* me.

Stevie (*short harsh chuckle*)   Don't mock *me*.

Martin   I . . . I went over to where she was – to the fence where she was, and I knelt there, eye level . . .

Stevie (*quiet loathing*)   *Goat* level.

Martin (*angry; didactic*)   I will *finish* this! You *asked* for it, and you're going to *get* it! So . . . shut your tragic mouth! (**Stevie** *does a sharp intake of breath, puts her fingers over her mouth.*) All right. Listen to me. It was as if an alien came out of whatever it was, and it . . . took me with it, and it was . . . an ecstasy and a purity, and a . . . love of a . . . (*dogmatic*) un-i-mag-in-able kind, and it relates to nothing *whatever*, to nothing that can be *related* to! Don't you see?! Don't you see the . . . don't you see the 'thing' that happened to me? What nobody understands? Why I can't feel what I'm supposed to?! Because it relates to nothing? It can't have happened! It did but it *can't* have! (**Stevie** *shakes her head.*) What are you doing?

Stevie (*removes fingers*) Being tragic. I bet a psychiatrist would love all of this. (*Replaces fingers.*)

Martin I knelt there, eye level, and there was a . . . a what?! . . . an understanding so intense, so natural . . .

Stevie There are some things you *can* remember, eh?

Martin (*closes his eyes, reopens them*) . . . an understanding so . . .

Stevie (*awful, high-pitched little voice*) I can't remember why I come into rooms, where I put the thing for the razor . . .

Martin (*refusing to be drawn in*) . . . an understanding so natural, so intense that I will *never* forget it, as intense as the night you and I finally came at the same time. What was it . . . a month after we began? (*Where is she, emotionally?*) Stevie? It wasn't happening . . . but it *was*!

Stevie (*shaking her head; oddly objective*) How *much* do you hate me?

Martin (*hopeless*) I *love* you. (*Pause.*) And I love *her*. (*Pause.*) And there it is.

Stevie *howls three times, slowly, deliberately; a combination of rage and hurt.*

Stevie (*calmly*) Go on.

Martin (*apologetic*) I have to do it.

Stevie   Yes? (**Martin** *nods.*) Right.

Martin (*starting again*)   And there was a connection there –
a communication – that, well . . . an epiphany, I guess
comes closest, and I knew what was going to happen.

Stevie (*mildly interested in the fact*)   I think I'm going to be
sick.

Martin   *Please* don't. (*Back to it.*) Epiphany! And when it
happens there's no retreating, no holding back. I put my
hands through the wires of the fence and she came towards
me, slipped her face between my hands, brought her nose to
mine at the wires and . . . and nuzzled.

Stevie   I am a grown woman; a grown married woman.
(*As if she's never heard the word before.*) Nuzzled; nuzzled.

Martin   Her breath . . . her breath was . . . so sweet,
warm and . . . (*Hears something; stops.*)

Stevie   Go on. Tell the grown-up married woman . . .

Martin (*warning hand up*)   I hear Billy.

Billy *enters.*

Billy   Are you hitting her?! (*Sees the carnage.*) What the fuck?!

Stevie   We're redecorating, honey. No, he's not, by the
way – hitting me. I'm hitting myself.

Billy (*near tears*)   I hear you two! I'm up there and I *hear*
you! STOP IT! JESUS GOD, STOP IT!

Martin (*gentle*)   We will, Billy; we're not quite done.

Stevie   Go away, Billy. Go out and play.

Billy   Go out and . . . ?

Stevie (*harder*)   Leave the house! Leave us alone!

Billy   But . . .

Martin (*calm*)   Do what your mother says. Go out and
play. Make mud pies; climb a tree . . .

Billy (*a finger in* **Martin**'s *face*)   If I come back and find you've hurt her, I'll . . . I'll . . . (*Weeps openly, sobs, runs from the room. We hear the front door slam.*)

Stevie (*after*)   Mud pies?

Martin   Well . . . whatever.

Stevie (*calm*)   What *will* you do if he comes back and finds you've hurt me? . . . *When* he comes back and finds you've hurt me?

Martin (*absorbed in something*)   What?

Stevie (*smiles*)   Down from the trees, hands all muddy? (*Sad.*) Nothing. (*Cold.*) You were in the middle of your epiphany.

Martin (*sighs*)   Yes.

Stevie (*sad*)   God, I wish you were stupid.

Martin (*he, too*)   Yes; I wish *you* were stupid, too.

Stevie (*pause; businesslike*)   Epiphany!

Martin   Yes. It was at that moment that I realised . . .

Stevie   . . . that you and the fucking goat were destined for one another!

Martin   . . . that she and I were . . . (*Softly; embarrassed.*) That she and I were going to bed together.

Stevie   To stall together! To hay! *Not* to bed!

Martin (*sits*)   Whatever. That what could not happen was *going* to. That we wanted each other very much, that I had to have her, that I . . . (**Stevie** *screams – a deep-throated rage – and lunges at* **Martin**. *He rises, grabs her wrists and shoves her into a chair. She attempts to get up, but he shoves her back again.*) Now stop it! Let me finish!

Stevie   You'll be fucking Billy next.

Martin (*ice*)   He's not my type.

Stevie (*rising again. Rage*)   He's not your type?! He's not your fucking type?!

Martin   No; he's not. (*She is about to strike him.*) *You're* my type. (*The shock of this stays her gesture; we see her confusion.*) *You're* my type.

Stevie (*stands where she is; hard*)   Thank you!

Martin   You're welcome. (*A gesture.*) Oh, Stevie, I . . .

Stevie   I'm your type and so is she; so is the goat. (*Harder.*) So long as it's female, eh? So long as it's got a cunt it's all right with you!

Martin (*huge*)   A SOUL! Don't you know the difference?! Not a cunt, a soul!

Stevie (*after a little; tears again*)   You can't fuck a soul.

Martin   No; and it isn't about fucking.

Stevie   YES!

Martin (*as gentle as possible*)   No; no, Stevie, it isn't.

Stevie (*pause; then, even more sure*)   Yes! It is about fucking! It is about you being an animal!

Martin (*thinks a moment; quietly*)   I thought I was.

Stevie (*contempt*)   Hunh!

Martin   I thought I was; I thought we *all* were . . . animals.

Stevie (*cold rage*)   We stay with our own kind!

Martin (*gentle; rational*)   Oh, we fall in love with *many* other creatures . . . dogs and cats, and . . .

Stevie   We don't *fuck* them! You're a monster!

Martin (*pinning it down*)   I am a deeply troubled, greatly divided . . .

Stevie (*no quarter*)   *Animal*-fucker!

Martin   Sylvia and I . . .

Stevie (*hideous*) You're going to tell me she *wants* you.

Martin (*simply put*) Yes.

Stevie What does she do – back into you making awful little bleating sounds?

Martin That's sheep.

Stevie *Whatever! Presented* herself? Down on her forelegs, her head turned, her eyes on you, her . . .

Martin Stop it! I won't go into the specifics of our sex with you!

Stevie (*contempt*) *Thank* you! You take advantage of this . . . creature?! You . . . *rape* this . . . animal and convince yourself that it has to do with *love*?!

Martin (*helpless*) I love her . . . and she loves me, and . . .

Stevie (*a huge animal sound: rage; sweeps the bookcase of whatever is on it, or overturns a piece of furniture. Silence; then starting quietly, building*) Now you listen to me. I have listened to you. I have heard you tell me how much you love me, how you've never even wanted another woman, how we have been a more perfect marriage than chance would even *allow*. We're both too bright for *most* of the shit. We see the deep and awful humour of things go over the heads of most people; we see what's hideously wrong in what most people accept as normal; we have both the joys and the sorrows of all that. We have a straight line through life, right all the way to dying, but that's okay because it's a good line . . . so long as we don't screw up.

Martin I know; I know.

Stevie (*don't interrupt me!*) Shut up; so long as we don't screw up. (*Points at him.*) And *you've* screwed *up*!

Martin Stevie, I . . .

Stevie I said, shut up. Do you know *how* you've done it? How you've screwed up?

Martin (*mumbled*)   Because I was at the vegetable stand one day, and I looked over to my right and I saw . . .

Stevie (*hard and slow*)   Because you've broken something and it can't be fixed!

Martin   Stevie . . .

Stevie   Fall out of love with me? Fine! No, not fine, but that can be fixed . . . time . . . whatever! But tell me you love me and an animal – both of us! – equally? The same way? That you go from my bed – *our* bed . . . (*Aside-ish.*) It's amazing, you know, how good we are, still, how we please each other *and* ourselves so . . . fully, so . . . fresh each time . . . (*Aside over.*) You go from our bed, wash your dick, get in your car and go to her, and do with her what I cannot imaging myself imagining? Or – worse! . . . that you've come *from* her, to *my* bed?! To *our* bed?! . . . and you do with me what I *can* imagine . . . love . . . *want* you for?!

Martin (*deep sadness*)   Oh, Stevie . . .

Stevie (*not listening*)   That you can do these two things . . . and not understand how it . . . SHATTERS THE GLASS?! How it cannot be dealt with – how stop and forgiveness have nothing to do with it? And how *I* am destroyed? How *you* are? How I cannot admit it though I *know* it?! How I cannot deny it because I cannot *admit* it?! Cannot admit it because it is outside of denying?!

Martin   Stevie, I . . . I promise you, I'll stop; I'll . . .

Stevie   How stopping has nothing to do with having started?! How nothing has anything to do with anything?! (*Tears – if there – stop.*) You have brought me down, you goat-fucker; you love of my life! You have brought me down to *nothing*! (*Accusatory finger right at him.*) You have brought me down, and, Christ!, I'll bring you down with me!

Brief pause; she turns on her heel, exits. We hear the front door slam.

Martin (*after she leaves; after he hears to door; little boy*)   Stevie? (*Pause.*) Stevie?

Scene Three

An hour or so later. **Martin** *is sitting in the ruins. Maybe he is examining a broken piece of something. The room is as it was at the end of Scene Two. The front door slams;* **Billy** *enters;* **Martin** *does not look up.*

Billy (*looking around*)   Wow!

Martin (*realising* **Billy** *is there*)   Yes; wow.

Billy (*seemingly casual; righting a chair, perhaps*)   You guys really had it out, hunh.

Martin (*subdued; almost laughing*)   Oh, yes.

Billy   Where is she?

Martin   Hm? Who?

Billy (*not friendly; overly articulated*)   My mother. Where is my mother?

Martin (*mocking*)   'Where is my mother'? Not 'Mother – where's Mother?' Not that, but . . . 'Where is my mother?'

Billy (*anger rising*)   Whatever! Where *is* she? Where is *my* Mother?

Martin (*arms out; helplessly*)   I . . . I . . .

Billy (*angrier*)   Where *is* she?! What did you do . . . kill her?

Martin (*softly*)   Yes; I think so.

Billy (*dropping something he has picked up*)   What?!

Martin (*quietly, with a restraining hand*)   Stop. No. No, I did not kill her – of *course* not – but I think I might as well have. I think we've killed each other.

Billy (*driving*)   Where *is* she?!

Martin (*simply*)   I don't know.

Billy   What do you mean you don't . . .

Martin (*loud*)   She left!

Billy   What do you mean she left? Where . . .

Martin (*snappish*)   Stop asking me what I mean! (*Quieter.*) She said what she wanted to say; she finished . . . and she left. She slammed the front door and left. I assume she drove somewhere.

Billy   Yeah, the wagon's gone. (*Harder.*) Where *is* she?!

Martin (*loud*)   She *left*! I don't know where she *is*! It's English! 'She left.' It's English. No, I did not kill her, yes, I think I did, I think we killed each other. That's English, too: one of your courses!

Billy (*is his rage close to tears? Probably*)   I know who you *are*. I know you're my father. I know who you are, and I know who you're supposed to be, but . . .

Martin   You too?

Billy   Hunh?

Martin   You don't know who I *am* any more.

Billy (*flat*)   No.

Martin   Well . . . neither does your mother.

Billy (*trying to explain but, still, rage underneath*)   Parents fight; I know that; all kids know that. There are good times and rotten ones, and sometimes the blanket is pulled out from under you, and . . .

Martin (*can't help saying it*)   You're mixing your metaphors.

Billy (*furious*)   What?!

Martin   Never mind; probably not the best time to bring it up. You were saying . . . 'there are good times and rotten ones'?

Billy   Yes. (*Quick sarcasm.*) Thanks.

Martin (*non-committal*)   Welcome.

Billy   But sometimes the whatever is pulled out from under you.

Martin   Rug, I think.

Billy   Right! Now shut the fuck up! (**Martin** *opens his mouth, closes it. Spat out.*) Semanticist!

Martin   Very good! Where did you learn that?

Billy   I go to a good school. Remember?

Martin   Yes, but still . . .

Billy   I said, shut the fuck up!

Martin (*subsiding*)   Right.

Billy   There are good times and there are rotten ones. There are times we are so . . . deep in content, in happiness, that we think we'll probably drown in it but we won't mind. There are *some* of those – not too many. There are times we don't know what the fuck's going on – *to* us, *with* us, *about* us – and that's most of the time. I'm talking about us so-called adolescents.

Martin   I know.

Billy   And then there are the times we wish we were old enough to . . . just walk out the door and start all over again, somewhere else – blank it all out.

Martin (*quietly*)   And this?

Billy (*hard*)   One guess, you *fuck*!! (*Huge.*) What have you done with my *mother*?!

Martin (*calm*)   We finished our conversation (*Gestures at the ruined room.*) – you see how we talk? – we finished our conversation, and she said a final . . . *thing*, and she left. She walked out, out the front door, slam.

Billy   How long ago?

Martin (*shrugs*)   An hour; maybe more; maybe two. I'm not very good at time and stuff right now.

Billy   Two hours? And you haven't . . .

Martin (*a little angry himself*)   What?! Called the police?
(*Awful imitation of distress.*) 'Oh, officer, help me! My wife just
found I've been doing it with livestock, and she's run off,
and can you help me find her?' What?! Take off after her?!
She's a grown woman; she could be having her hair done,
for all I know.

Billy (*dogged*)   What did she *say* to you?

Martin (*rueful chuckle*)   Oh . . . quite a few things.

Billy (*bigger*)   When she left! What did she say when she
left?!

Martin   Something about . . . bringing me down – or
whatever.

Billy   Be specific.

Martin   Well, it's hard to be specific. We *were* busy after
all, and . . .

Billy (*big*)   Exactly what she said, and *now*!

Martin (*clears his throat*)   'You have brought me down, and
. . . I will bring you down with me.'

Billy (*puzzled; trying to get it*)   What does that *mean*?

Martin (*almost sweet*)   No one's ever brought you down?
No, I suppose not – not yet. It means . . . (*Fails.*) It means
what it says: that you have done to me what cannot be
undone and . . . and you won't get away with it.

Billy *stands for a moment and then spontaneously cries for a little,
stops.*

Billy (*wiping his eyes*)   I see.

Martin (*further explanation*)   You destroy me – I destroy
you.

Billy   Yes; I see. (*Indicates wreckage.*) Then there's no point
in setting all this right.

Martin (*sad chuckle*)   It does look pretty awful, *doesn't* it.

Billy   Let's do it anyway.

Martin   Set the stage for the next round? (*Some self-pity and irony.*) Hunh! *What* next round?! It's all behind me, isn't it? – everything? All hope . . . all . . . 'salvation'? (*Fast litany.*) Dead-end-rock-bottom-out-with-the-garbage-flushed-down-the-toilet-ground-up-spit-out-over-the-edge with heavy weights, down-down-sunk . . . whatever? All hope, everything? Gone? Right?

Billy (*shrugs*)   Whatever. (*They begin to right a few things, not much.*) What is it going to be then? Divorce?

Martin (*simply*)   I don't know, Billy; I don't know that there are any rules for where we are.

Billy   Beyond all the rules, eh?

Martin (*some rue*)   I think so.

Billy   I wouldn't know. I guess I've never been in love. *Yet*, I mean. Oh, lots of crushes, and all.

Martin   Only twice for me – your mother and . . . Sylvia.

Billy   You're really holding onto this, *aren't* you.

Martin   To . . . ?

Billy (*sneering*)   This goat! This big love affair!

Martin (*shrugs*)   It's true.

Billy   Grow up!

Martin   Ah! Is *that* it! (**Billy** *laughs, in spite of himself.* **Martin** *tries to right a table.*)   Help me with this. (*Oddly offended.*) Thanks!

Billy (*shrugs*)   Any time. (*Pause.*) They asked us at school – when? Last week, last month? – they asked each of us in this class to talk about how normal our lives were, how . . . how conventional it all was and how did we feel about it.

Martin   What kind of school *is* this?!

Billy (*shrugs*)   You chose it; you two chose it. And a lot of
the guys got up and talked about – you know – our home
lives, how our parents get on, and all; and it wasn't very
special except the guys whose parents are divorced or one
has died or gone crazy, or whatever.

Martin   Really? Crazy?

Billy   Sure. Good private school. All guys, too; thanks. I
mean, it was all about what you'd expect. Maybe everybody
left all the juicy stuff out, or they didn't know it. (*Picks up a
shard.*) Where does this go?

Martin   Trash, I suspect.

Billy (*looks at it*)   Too bad. (*Drops it.*) So, it was all pretty
dull, pretty much what you'd expect.

Martin   I take it you haven't gotten up and spoken yet.

Billy (*non-committal*)   Nope. Haven't. (*Waits a little.*) You
know what I'm going to tell them – when I get up there on
my hind legs?

Martin (*winces*)   Do I *want* to know?

Billy   Sure; you're a big guy.

Martin   I am diminished.

Billy   Yeah? Well . . . whatever. I think what I'll tell is this:
that I've been living with two people about as splendid as
you can get; that if I'd been born to other people it couldn't
have been any better. (**Martin** *sighs heavily, puts a protesting
hand up.*) No; really; I mean it. You two guys are about as
good as they come. You're smart, and fair, and you have a
sense of humour – both of you – and . . . and you're
Democrats. You *are* Democrats, aren't you?

Martin   More than *they* are, sometimes.

Billy   That's what I thought, and you've figured out that
raising a kid does *not* include making him into a carbon copy

of *you*, that you're letting me think you're putting up with me being gay far better than you probably really are.

Martin   Oh, now . . .

Billy   Thank you, by the way.

Martin   It's the least.

Billy (*nodding*)   Right.

Martin (*feigned surprise*)   You're *gay*?!

Billy (*smiles*)   Shut up. Anyway, you've let me have it better than a lot of kids, better than a lot of 'moms and dads' have, a lot closer to what being grown up will look like – as far as I can tell. Good guidance; it's great to see how two people can love each other . . .

Martin   Don't!

Billy   At least that's what I thought – until today, until the shit hit the fan!

Martin   Billy, please don't.

Billy (*big crying underneath*)   . . . Until the shit hit the fan, and the talk I was going to do at school became history. (*Exaggerated.*) What will I say *now*?! Goodness me! The Good Ship Lollipop has gone and sunk. (*More normal tone.*) What will I say?! Well, let's see: I came home yesterday and everything had been great – absolutely normal, therefore great. Great parents, great house, great trees, great cars – you know: the old 'great'. (*Bigger now, more exaggerated.*) But then today I come home and what do I *find*? I find my great mom and my great dad talking about a letter from great good friend Ross . . .

Martin (*deep anger*)   Fuck Ross!

Billy   Yes? A letter from great good friend Ross written to great good Mom about how great good Dad has been out in the barnyard fucking *animals*!

Martin   Don't . . . *do* this.

Billy   Animals! Well, one in particular. A goat! A fucking goat! You see, guys, your stories are swell or whatever, but I've got one'll knock your socks off, as they used to say, wipe the tattoos right off your butts. Ya see, while great old Mom and great old Dad have been doing the great old parent thing, one of them has been underneath the house, down in the cellar, digging a pit so deep!, so wide!, so . . . HUGE! . . . we'll all fall in and (*Crying now.*) and never . . . be . . . able . . . to . . . climb . . . out . . . again – no matter how much we want to, how hard we try. And you see, kids, fellow students, you see, I love these people. I love the man who's been down there digging – when he's not giving it to a goat! I love this man! I love him! (*Drops whatever he's holding, moves to* **Martin**, *arms out.*) I love him!

Billy *wraps his arms around* **Martin**, *who doesn't know what to do. He starts kissing* **Martin** *on the hands, then on the neck, crying all the while. Then it turns – or does it? – and he kisses* **Martin** *full on the mouth – a deep, sobbing, sexual kiss.* **Ross** *enters, stands watching.* **Martin** *tries to disengage from* **Billy**, *but* **Billy** *moans, holds on. Finally* **Martin** *shoves him away.* **Billy** *stands there, still sobbing, arms around nothing. They have not seen* **Ross**.

Martin   Don't *do* that!!

Billy   I *love* you!

Martin   Sure you do, you . . . you . . .

Billy   Faggot? You faggot?

Martin (*enraged*)   That's not what I was going to say!

Billy (*so sad; so sincere*)   Dad! I *love* you! Hold me! Please!

Martin (*holds him; strokes him*)   Shhhhhh; shhhh; shhhhh now.

Billy (*disengaging finally*)   I'm sorry; I didn't mean to . . .

Martin   No; it's all right. (*Arms out.*) Here; let me hold you.

Billy *moves to him again; a momentary silent embrace.*

Ross   Excuse me. (*They are startled, split. Maybe* **Billy** *stumbles over something.*) I'm sorry; I didn't mean to interrupt your little . . .

Martin (*cold fury*)   What?! See a man and his son kissing? That would go nicely in one of your fucking letters. Judas! Get out of here!

Billy (*to* **Ross**)   It wasn't what you think!

Martin (*at* **Billy**)   Yes! Yes, it was! Don't apologise. (*To* **Ross**.) Too bad you couldn't have brought your fucking TV crew over! Don't you and *your* son ever kiss? Don't you and – what's his name? – *Todd* love one another?

Ross (*hard; contemptuous*)   Not *that* way!

Martin (*angry and reckless*)   *That* way?! *What* way?! (*Points vigorously at* **Billy**.) This boy is hurt! I've hurt him and he still loves me! You fucker! He loves his father, and if it . . . clicks over and becomes – what? – sexual for . . . just a moment . . . so what?! So fucking what?! He's hurt and he's lonely and mind your own fucking business!

Ross (*a sneer*)   You're sicker than I thought.

Martin   No! I'm hysterical!

Billy (*rueful wonder*)   It *did*. It clicked over, and you were just another . . .

Martin   It's all right.

Billy   . . . another man. I get confused . . . sex and love; loving and . . . (*To* **Ross**.) I probably *do* want to sleep with him. (*Rueful laugh.*) I want to sleep with everyone.

Martin (*to quiet him*)   It's all right.

Billy (*still to* **Ross**)   Except you, probably.

Ross   Jesus! Sick! What is it . . . contagious?

Billy (*confused*)   What? Is what?

Martin (*moves over to comfort* **Billy**)   There was a man told
me once – a friend; we went to the same gym – he told me
he had his kid on his lap one day – not even old enough to
be a boy or a girl: a baby – and he had . . . *it* on his lap, and
it was gurgling at him and making giggling sounds, and he
had it with his arms around it (*Demonstrates.*) in his lap,
shifting it a little from side to side to make it happier, to
make it giggle more . . . and all at once he realised he was
getting hard.

Ross   Jesus!

Billy   Oh my God . . .

Martin   . . . That the baby in his lap was making him
hard – not arousing him; it wasn't sexual, but it was
happening.

Ross   Jesus!

Martin   . . . His dick was rising to the baby in his lap – his
baby; his lap. And when he realised what was happening, he
thought he would die; his pulse was going a mile a minute;
his ears were ringing – loud! Very *loud*! And he was going to
faint; he *knew* it, and then the moment passed and he knew
it had all been an accident, that it meant . . . nothing – that
nothing was connected to anything else. His wife came in;
she smiled; he smiled and handed her the baby. And that
was it; it was over. (*Shrugs.*) Things happen. Besides – I'm
hysterical. Remember?

Ross   What are you doing? *Defending* yourself?! Jesus.
You're sick.

Martin (*contempt*)   Do you have any other words? Sick and
Jesus? Is that all you have? (*Turning to* **Ross**.) So, what do
you want here now, motherfucker?! Judas?!

Ross   Stevie called – what? An hour ago? More? She said
you needed me; she said to come over.

Martin   I don't! Get out! (*Surprise.*) She *called* you?

Ross   Yes. (*Shakes his head.*) Getting hard with a baby! Is there anything you people don't get off on?!

Martin (*to* **Ross**; *hard, eyes narrowing*)   Is there anything 'we people' don't get off on? Is there anything anyone doesn't get off on, whether we admit it or not – whether we *know* it or not? Remember Saint Sebastian with all the arrows shot into him? He probably came! God knows the faithful did! Shall I go on?! You want to hear about the cross?!

Ross (*shaking his head; sad, but with a lip curled*)   Sick; sick; sick.

Martin (*at* **Ross**; *growing rage*)   I'll tell you what's sick! Writing that fucking letter to Stevie – why doesn't matter! – that's what's sick! I *tell* you about it; I share it with you, the . . . the . . . whole . . . awful . . . thing, because I think I've lost it, maybe; I *tell* you; I *share* it with you because you're . . . what?! . . . you're my best friend in the whole world? Because I needed to tell *somebody*, somebody with his head on straight enough to hear it? I *tell* you, and you fucking turn around and . . .

Ross (*dogmatic*)   I couldn't let you *continue*!

Martin (*near tears*)   I could have worked it out. I could have stopped, and no one would have known. Except you, motherfucker. Mister one strike and you're out. I could have . . .

Ross   No! You couldn't!

Martin   I could have worked it out! And now nothing can *ever* be put back together! *Ever*!

Billy (*trying to help*)   Dad . . .

Martin (*savage*)   You shut up! (**Billy** *winces.* **Martin** *reacts.*) Oh, God! I'm sorry. (*To* **Ross**.) Yes; all right, it *was* sick, and yes, it *was* compulsive, and . . .

Ross   IS! Not *was*! IS!

Martin (*stopped in his tracks*)   I . . . I . . .

Ross IS!

Martin (*gathering himself*)   *Is*. All right. *Is. Is* sick; *is* compulsive.

Ross (*pushing*)   And it was *wrong*!

Martin It was . . . it was . . . what?

Ross Wrong! Deeply, destructively *wrong*!

Martin Whatever you want. (*Rage growing.*) But I could have handled it! You didn't have to bring it all down! You didn't have to destroy both of us; you didn't have to destroy Stevie, too!

Ross Me?! *Me* bring you down?! This isn't . . . embezzlement, honey; this isn't stealing from helpless widows; this isn't going to whores and coming down with the clap, or whatever, you know. This isn't the stuff that stops a career in its tracks for a little while – humiliation, public remorse, and then back up again. This is *beyond* that – *way* beyond it! You go on and you'll slip up one day. Somebody'll see you. Somebody'll surprise you one day, in whatever barn you put her in, no matter where you put her. Somebody'll see you, on your knees behind the damn animal; your pants around your ankles. Somebody will *catch* you at it.

Billy Let him alone. For God's sake, Ross . . .

Ross (*waving* **Billy** *off; to* **Martin**)   Do you know what they'd *do* to you? The press? Everybody? Down it all comes – your career; your life . . . everything. (*So cold; so rational.*) For fucking a goat. (*Shakes his head sadly;* **Billy** *is weeping quietly.*)

Martin (*long pause*)   Is *that* what it is, then? That people will *know*?! That people will find *out*?! That I can do whatever I want, and that's what matters?! That people will find *out*?! Fuck the . . . thing it*self*?! Fuck what it *means*?! That people will find *out*?!

Ross   Your soul is your own business. The rest I can *help* you with.

Martin   Of course it's my business, and clearly you don't have one.

Ross (*mild interest*)   Oh?

Martin   So that's what it comes down to, eh? . . . what we can get away with?

Ross   Sure.

Martin (*heavy irony*)   Oh, thank God! It's so simple! I thought it was . . . I thought it had to do with love and loss, and it's only about . . . getting *by*. Well, Stevie and I have been wrestling with the wrong angel! When she comes back – *if* she comes back – I'll have to set her straight about what matters. (*Intense; not looking at* **Ross** *or* **Billy***; pounding his hands on his knees, perhaps.*) Does nobody understand what happened?!

Ross   Oh, for Christ's sake, Martin!

Billy   Dad . . .

Martin (*crying a little*)   Why can't anyone understand this . . . that I am *alone* . . . all . . . *alone*?!

A silence. Then we hear a sound at the door.

Billy   Mom? (**Billy** *going into what's left of the hall. Gone.*)

Martin (*pause; to* **Ross***, begging*)   You *do* understand; *don't* you?

Ross (*long pause; shakes his head*)   No.

Stevie *enters, dragging a dead goat. The goat's throat is cut; the blood is down* **Stevie***'s dress, on her arms. She stops.*

Ross   Oh, my God.

Martin   What have you done?!

Stevie   Here.

Billy (*generally; to no one; helpless; a quiet plea*)   Help. Help.

Ross   Oh, my God.

Martin *moves towards* **Stevie**.

Martin   What have you done?! Oh, my God, what have you *done*?!

Stevie (*turns to face him; evenly, without emotion*)   I went where Ross told me I would find . . . your friend. I found her. I killed her. I brought her here to you. (*Odd little question.*) No?

Martin (*a profound cry*)   ANNNNNNH!

Stevie   Why are you surprised? What did you expect me to do?

Martin (*crying*)   What did she *do*?! What did she ever *do*?! (*To* **Stevie**.) I ask you: what did she ever *do*?!

Stevie (*pause; quietly*)   She loved you . . . you say. As much as *I* do.

Martin (*to* **Stevie**; *empty*)   I'm sorry. (*To* **Billy**; *empty*.) I'm sorry. (*Then . . .*) I'm sorry.

Billy (*to one, then the other; no reaction from them*)   Dad? Mom?

Tableau.

Methuen Modern Plays

include work by

Edward Albee
Jean Anouilh
John Arden
Margaretta D'Arcy
Peter Barnes
Sebastian Barry
Brendan Behan
Dermot Bolger
Edward Bond
Bertolt Brecht
Howard Brenton
Anthony Burgess
Simon Burke
Jim Cartwright
Caryl Churchill
Noël Coward
Lucinda Coxon
Sarah Daniels
Nick Darke
Nick Dear
Shelagh Delaney
David Edgar
David Eldridge
Dario Fo
Michael Frayn
John Godber
Paul Godfrey
David Greig
John Guare
Peter Handke
David Harrower
Jonathan Harvey
Iain Heggie
Declan Hughes
Terry Johnson
Sarah Kane
Charlotte Keatley
Barrie Keeffe
Howard Korder

Robert Lepage
Doug Lucie
Martin McDonagh
John McGrath
Terrence McNally
David Mamet
Patrick Marber
Arthur Miller
Mtwa, Ngema & Simon
Tom Murphy
Phyllis Nagy
Peter Nichols
Sean O'Brien
Joseph O'Connor
Joe Orton
Louise Page
Joe Penhall
Luigi Pirandello
Stephen Poliakoff
Franca Rame
Mark Ravenhill
Philip Ridley
Reginald Rose
Willy Russell
Jean-Paul Sartre
Sam Shepard
Wole Soyinka
Shelagh Stephenson
Peter Straughan
C. P. Taylor
Theatre de Complicite
Theatre Workshop
Sue Townsend
Judy Upton
Timberlake Wertenbaker
Roy Williams
Snoo Wilson
Victoria Wood

Methuen Contemporary Dramatists
include

John Arden (two volumes)
Arden & D'Arcy
Peter Barnes (three volumes)
Sebastian Barry
Dermot Bolger
Edward Bond (six volumes)
Howard Brenton
(two volumes)
Richard Cameron
Jim Cartwright
Caryl Churchill (two volumes)
Sarah Daniels (two volumes)
Nick Darke
David Edgar (three volumes)
Ben Elton
Per Olov Enquist
Dario Fo (two volumes)
Michael Frayn (three volumes)
David Greig
John Godber (two volumes)
Paul Godfrey
John Guare
Lee Hall (two volumes)
Peter Handke
Jonathan Harvey
(two volumes)
Declan Hughes
Terry Johnson (two volumes)
Sarah Kane
Barrie Keefe
Bernard-Marie Koltès
David Lan
Bryony Lavery
Deborah Levy
Doug Lucie

David Mamet (four volumes)
Martin McDonagh
Duncan McLean
Anthony Minghella
(two volumes)
Tom Murphy (four volumes)
Phyllis Nagy
Anthony Neilsen
Philip Osment
Louise Page
Stewart Parker (two volumes)
Joe Penhall
Stephen Poliakoff
(three volumes)
David Rabe
Mark Ravenhill
Christina Reid
Philip Ridley
Willy Russell
Eric-Emmanuel Schmitt
Ntozake Shange
Sam Shepard (two volumes)
Martin Sherman
Shelagh Stephenson
Wole Soyinka (two volumes)
David Storey (three volumes)
Sue Townsend
Judy Upton
Michel Vinaver
(two volumes)
Arnold Wesker (two volumes)
Michael Wilcox
Roy Williams
Snoo Wilson (two volumes)
David Wood (two volumes)
Victoria Wood

For a complete catalogue of Methuen Drama titles
write to:

Methuen Drama
215 Vauxhall Bridge Road
London SW1V 1EJ

or you can visit our website at:

www.methuen.co.uk